Vegan Indoor Grill Cookbook for Beginners 2021

365-Day New Tasty Plant-Based Recipes for Mouthwatering Vegetarian Grilling | Help You Lose Weight, Be Healthier, and Feel Better Every Day

Ermy Kony

Table of contents

Introduction

If you are looking for a healthier way to make indoor grilled foods, if you are wanting to add more plants to your diet, then you have come to the right place. You are going to find hundreds of plant-based recipes that you can whip up for your next indoor grill. Indoor grill has never been so quick, diverse, or delicious. Vegetables cooked on the indoor grill take on a sweet taste that's irresistible.

Vegan diet doesn't mean you have to settle for a life without comfort food! This cookbook will take your grill skills to a whole new level. You will get many choices into vegan for keeping slim and feeling better. Vegan Indoor Grill Cookbook for Beginners 2021 is all you need to create the vegan indoor grill meals of your dreams.

This cookbook has everything you need to have a great vegan indoor grill meal. You'll learn how to cook healthy and tasty vegan delicacies by following the grilling instructions to grill easily, smartly and speedily.

Chapter 1: Vegetable Recipes

Cucumber Salad

A fresh cucumber salad is impressive, unique and a great addition to a party on a hot summer's day.

Ingredients:

For the Dressing:

- 2 Tbsp raw cashews, soaked overnight
- 2 Tbsp pine nuts, soaked overnight
- 1/2 Tbsp brown rice syrup (see notes for substitutions)
- 1½ Tbsp fresh lemon juice
- 1 cucumber, peeled
- Salt and pepper, to taste
- 1-2 tsp water

Instructions:

1. Combine all dressing ingredients in a blender or food processor and blend/process until smooth.

For the Cucumber Salad:

- 4 cucumbers, sliced thinly
- Salt
- 1 18-oz can chickpeas, rinsed and drained
- 1/4 cup red onion, sliced thin
- 1/4 cup fresh dill, chopped
- Salt and pepper, to taste
- Smoked paprika, for garnish

Instructions:

1. In a colander, toss your 4 sliced cucumbers with some salt. Let drain for about 20 minutes, stirring around a few times to draw as much moisture out as possible.
2. Now rinse the salt off the cucumbers with cold water and pat dry. (You could use a salad spinner if you have one.)

3. Prepare the Dressing
4. Combine all dressing ingredients in a blender or food processor and blend/process until smooth.

Assemble the Salad:

In a large bowl, combine cucumbers, chickpeas, red onion and dill. Add in the dressing, mixing until everything is well-combined. Adjust seasonings as needed.
Refrigerate until ready to eat. Serve cold.

Summer Bowtie Pasta Salad

I like a good chilled pasta salad. Feel free to substitute a different kind of pasta, but I just love a fresh bow tie pasta salad.

Ingredients:

- 12 oz. bow tie pasta, cooked according to package instructions
- 1/2 bunch parsley, stems removed
- 2 plum tomatoes, diced
- 1 summer squash, diced
- 1 zucchini, diced
- 1 broccoli crown, diced
- 1/2 red onion, finely diced
- 2/3 of a 15-oz jar of roasted red peppers, diced

For the Vinaigrette:

- 1/4 cup peanut or canola oil
- 1/4 cup olive oil
- 1/3 cup red wine vinegar
- 1 Tbsp dijon mustard
- 1 tsp dried oregano
- 1 tsp minced garlic
- 3/4 tsp salt
- Black pepper, to taste

Instructions:

1. Combine the vinaigrette ingredients in a bowl and whisk until well-combined.
2. In a bowl, combine the cooked pasta, your vegetables and the vinaigrette. Stir gently until everything is covered with the vinaigrette. Adjust seasonings to taste.
3. Refrigerate until ready to eat. Serve cold or at room temperature.

Beef Tomato Sheep's Cheese

Ingredients:

- 50 g butter
- 3 cloves of garlic
- 4 beefsteak tomatoes
- 200g sheep cheese

Instructions:

1. Wash beefsteak tomatoes and cut off the lid.
2. Hollow out the meat from the tomato.
3. Peel and press the garlic.
4. Mix the sheep's cheese with the garlic and butter.
5. Put the mixture in the tomatoes.
6. Put the cover back on.
7. Grill tomatoes over indirect heat and 160-180°C for 20 minutes.
8. It is important that the tomatoes are covered so that they can cook evenly.

Mushroom Cheese

Ingredients:

- 200g Gouda
- 1 tbsp olive oil
- 500 g mushrooms
- 2 onions
- 1 teaspoon parsley
- Salt
- Pepper

Instructions:

1. Clean the mushrooms, cut off the end of the stems.
2. Chop stalks into small pieces.
3. Peel the onion and cut into cubes.
4. Wash the parsley, pat dry and chop finely.
5. Rasp cheese.
6. Mix the mushroom stalks, salt, pepper, parsley, oil and onions and fill the mushrooms with it.
7. Scatter cheese on top.
8. Put the mushrooms in a grill basket.
9. Grill over indirect heat for 20 minutes.

French Fries

Ingredients:

- 2 tbsp paprika powder
- 500 g potatoes
- 3 tbsp olive oil
- Salt

Instructions:

1. Peel the potatoes and cut into strips of French fries.
2. Wash to remove the starch. Rub dry well.
3. Put salt, oil and paprika in a bowl. Add potatoes and mix well.
4. Place the fries in a grill pan or on a grill plate.
5. Grill with the lid closed for 30 minutes.

Corn On the Cob

Ingredients:

- 50g herb butter
- 4 ears of corn

Instructions:

1. Remove the leaves and threads from the corn.
2. Boil the corn on the cob in hot water for 20 minutes.
3. Pierce lengthways with a skewer.
4. Cook the corn on the grill for 10 minutes, turning.
5. Brush with herb butter before serving.

Artichoke and Rocket Onions

Ingredients:

- 200g rocket
- 12 artichoke hearts, pickled
- 1 clove of garlic
- 3 onions, red
- Juice of one lemon
- 50 mlof olive oil
- Salt
- Pepper

Instructions:

1. Drain the artichoke hearts.
2. Mix the lemon juice with the artichokes in a bowl.
3. Finely chop the garlic and mix with olive oil.
4. Peel the onions and cut into quarters.
5. Put the onions with the artichokes in an aluminum dish and place on the grill.
6. Drizzle everything with the garlic oil.
7. Grill the artichokes over medium heat for 15 minutes.
8. Wash the rocket and arrange on a plate. Place onions and artichokes on top.

Watermelon-Avocado-Tofu Ceviche

This is a unique dish featuring watermelon and tofu. Perfect for summer time.

Ingredients:

For Tofu Ceviche:

- Juice of 1 lime
- Juice of 1/2 orange, plus 1 Tbsp of orange zest
- Juice of 1/2 lemon
- 1/2 inch piece of ginger, grated or microplaned
- 1 red chile pepper, minced
- 2 Tbsp melted Earth Balance® Organic Coconut Spread
- 1 tsp sriracha sauce
- 1/2 tsp sea salt
- 1 14 oz package of extra firm tofu, pressed, drained and cut into 1-inch cubes

For the Salad:

- 2 avocados, diced
- 1 small watermelon, diced
- 1 cucumber, diced
- 1 bunch watercress
- 3 Tbsp fresh cilantro, chopped
- 2 Tbsp chives, chopped
- Salt
- Olive oil

Instructions:

1. Combine the tofu ceviche ingredients in a shallow container and let marinate for 1-2 hours in the fridge.
2. In a large bowl, combine the tofu ceviche with the Salad ingredients, and toss gently, taking care not to damage the tofu cubes or the avocado chunks.
3. Drizzle lightly with the olive oil and salt, and serve.

Grilled Zucchini

A nice little zucchini recipe, with a basic vinaigrette. This makes a good side dish.

Ingredients:

- 2 zucchinis, rinsed and patted dry
- 1/4 cup olive oil
- 1/4 balsamic vinegar
- 1/2 tsp sugar
- 1/2 tsp Italian seasoning
- Pepper, to taste

Instructions:

1. Slice each zucchini in half lengthwise, then in half lengthwise again, so that you have 8 slices of flat or flat-ish pieces.
2. In a small bowl, combine oil, vinegar, sugar, Italian seasoning and pepper and mix with a fork.
3. Add this marinade along with the zucchini into a plastic zipper bag and shake to combine. Let marinate in the refrigerator for about 30 minutes.
4. Preheat your grill to medium-high and lightly oil the grill rack.
5. Grill zucchini for about 2 minutes per side, until you have some nice grill arks and the zucchini has softened. Serve warm.

Grilled Corn

Grilled corn can only be made better by an elote sauce, which we will add at the end of this recipe.

Ingredients:

- 4 ears of corn on the cob, husked
- 1/2 cup vegan mayo
- 1/4 cup chopped fresh cilantro
- Juice from 1 lime
- Cayenne pepper

Vegan Parmesan :

(Pulse the below ingredients in a blender or food processor until it reaches a fine grain.)
- 1/2 cup cashews
- 2 Tbsp nutritional yeast
- 1/2 tsp salt
- 1/4 tsp garlic powder

Instructions:

1. Preheat grill to medium heat.
2. In a small bowl, combine the vegan mayo, cilantro, lime juice, cayenne pepper and vegan Parmesan.
3. Wrap each ear of corn in aluminum foil and place on the grill. Grill for about 15 minutes, turning regularly. Remove corn from the grill, unwrap and slather with the mayo mixture. Serve immediately.

Grilled Eggplant

Basic grilled eggplant makes for another nice side dish.

Ingredients:

- 1 eggplant, sliced into 1/2-inch-thick rounds
- 3 Tbsp olive oil
- Kosher salt

Instructions:

1. Preheat grill to medium-high heat.
2. Brush or spray both sides of each eggplant slice with salt and olive oil. Grill uncovered for about 4 minutes per side, until tender and you have some nice grill marks.
3. Serve.

Grilled Napa Cabbage

Another grilled vegetable. I never thought napa cabbage would come out so well on a grill. Make sure you char this nicely, as that brings out a ton of flavor.

Ingredients:

- 3 Tbsp hot Chinese mustard
- 1 Tbsp agave nectar
- 1 tsp olive oil + 2 tsp olive oil
- 1/4 tsp finely grated garlic
- 2 Tbsp fresh basil leaves, chopped
- 2 heads of napa cabbage, cut lengthwise into quarters
- 1 bunch of green onions

Instructions:

1. Preheat grill to high heat. In a small bowl, combine the mustard, agave nectar, 1 tsp oil, garlic and basil. Brush the cabbage quarters and green onions with the remaining olive oil.
2. Grill cabbage, flat side down, for about 3 minutes. Flip and cook another 3 minutes, until nicely charred.
3. Place green onions on grill and cook about 2 minutes, flipping halfway through.
4. Remove from heat, and brush the mustard sauce on the cabbage and green onions. Cut scallions into quarters and serve atop the grilled cabbage.

Grilled Asparagus

Another basic grilled vegetable recipe to serve as a side.

Ingredients:

- 1 pound asparagus, trimmed
- 3 Tbsp balsamic vinegar
- 2 Tbsp lemon juice
- 1 Tbsp olive oil
- 1 Tbsp soy sauce
- 1/8 tsp pepper

Instructions:

1. Preheat grill to medium heat and lightly oil the grill rack.
2. Combine vinegar, lemon juice, olive oil, soy sauce, pepper and add to a plastic zip bag with the asparagus. Let marinate for 30 minutes.
3. Grill asparagus, cooking each side for 5 minutes, until nicely charred.
4. Serve warm.

Grilled Artichokes

Artichokes have hard exteriors and take a bit of work to prepare, but they are worth it in the end. Just take it slow and make sure not to cut yourself.

Ingredients:

- 3 globe artichokes
- 1 lemon, cut into wedges
- 1/3 cup olive oil
- 1/2 Tbsp oregano
- 1/2 Tbsp thyme
- Salt, to taste

Instructions:

1. In a small saucepan, heat olive oil over medium-low heat, and add in the oregano and thyme until warmed through. Remove from heat and set aside to allow herbs to integrate into the oil.
2. Cut off and discard the top half-inch of the artichokes. Slice the artichokes in half lengthwise. Remove and discard the tough outer layers of the artichoke, and scoop out the small inner leaves and discard.
3. Rub lemon juice all over the inside and any area where cuts have been made.
4. Set up a pot with a steamer tray and a few inches of water. Bring water to a boil.
5. Reduce heat to medium and place the artichokes flat side down on the steamer tray. Steam for about 20 minutes.
6. Preheat grill to high heat.
7. Remove artichokes from steamer, and salt and brush all over with the herb-infused oil.
8. Grill flat side-down for 5-10 minutes, until nicely charred.
9. Remove from heat, sprinkle with lemon juice and serve warm with vegan mayo or aioli of your choosing.

Asparagus Halloumi

Ingredients:

- 1 clove of garlic
- 500g asparagus, green
- Juice of one lemon
- 250g halloumi
- Olive oil
- Salt
- Pepper
- Parsley

Instructions:

1. Peel garlic and chop finely.
2. Mix the lemon juice, salt, olive oil, pepper and garlic.
3. Wash the asparagus and cut the ends.
4. Put the asparagus in a bowl and add the lemon marinade.
5. Cut the halloumi into thin slices.
6. Preheat the grill plate.
7. Grill the asparagus and halloumi for a few minutes until the color changes slightly.
8. Put on the lid and grill indirectly for 15 minutes.
9. Finely chop the parsley and sprinkle on top.

Italian Eggplant "Sausages"

This recipe substitutes cooked eggplants for sausages which, let's be honest, is about a million times healthier.

Ingredients:

- 1/4 cup olive oil + 1 Tbsp
- 6 long Japanese eggplants, peeled
- 1 tsp ground fennel (optional)
- 1 tsp red pepper flakes
- 1 tsp rubbed sage
- 1 tsp Italian seasoning
- 2 tsp kosher salt
- 1/2 tsp black pepper
- 1/2 tsp onion powder
- 1/2 tsp garlic powder
- 6 hoagie rolls (or hot dog buns if you're in a pinch)
- 2 yellow onions, sliced thinly
- 2 bell peppers (any color), sliced thinly
- Mustard

Instructions:

1. In a large bowl, pour your olive oil over the peeled eggplants and rub it in. In a small bowl, combine fennel (if using), red pepper flakes, sage, Italian seasoning, salt, pepper, onion powder and garlic powder. Then rub this spice mixture into each eggplant.
2. Place eggplants in the fridge and let marinate for at least an hour.
3. While eggplants are marinating, make your onions and peppers. In a pan over medium heat, heat 1 Tbsp olive oil. Add in onions and peppers and cook for 7-8 minutes, until softened and starting to brown. Add salt and pepper to taste and remove from heat. Set aside.
4. After your eggplants have marinated, prepare your grill on medium heat. Cook eggplant for about 6 minutes per side, until you see some good grill marks on them, flipping once.
5. Place eggplant in warmed hoagie rolls, and garnish with onions and peppers and plenty of mustard.

Vegan Hot Dog

Yes, you can make vegan hot dogs on your own! This is a two-step cooking process, first steaming, then grilling the hot dogs.

Ingredients:

- 5 Tbsp almond meal
- 9 oz firm tofu
- 2 Tbsp soy sauce
- 3 Tbsp vegetable oil
- 1/2 medium onion, diced
- 2 cloves garlic, minced
- 1 Tbsp smoked paprika
- 1½ tsp granulated sugar
- 1 tsp salt
- 3/4 tsp ground black pepper
- 1 tsp ground coriander
- 1 tsp ground mustard
- 1/2 tsp nutmeg
- 1/2 tsp ground cardamom
- 1 tsp cumin
- 1 1/8 cup vital wheat gluten
- 1 tsp cornstarch

Instructions:

1. Using your hands, crumble the tofu into the bowl of your food processor. Add in the soy sauce and 1/3 cup water.
2. Add in the almond meal, oil, onion, garlic, paprika, sugar, salt, pepper, coriander, mustard, nutmeg, cardamom and cumin. Pulse until everything is smooth and well-combined. Transfer to a large mixing bowl.
3. Stir in the vital wheat gluten and cornstarch. Knead the dough until the mixture starts to develop strands from the addition of the wheat gluten. Don't go too far past this stage, as we don't want to over-knead the dough.
4. Divide the mixture into 8 pieces, rolling each piece into a hot dog shape. Wrap each hot dog in parchment paper, and then in aluminum foil, twisting the ends of the foil to close it off.
5. Now steam the hot dogs in a large pot with a steamer tray or rack.

6. Cover and steam for 45 minutes. Remove from heat and uncover, letting the hot dogs cool off by themselves.
7. Preheat your grill to medium-high heat, and grill the hot dogs for 4 minutes per side, until you have some nice grill marks.
8. Serve in a bun with normal hot dog toppings - mustard, relish, ketchup, chopped onions - whatever you like!

Grilled Veggie Pizza

Pizza tastes great grilled, mostly due to the fact that you can get a grill really, really hot. For this recipe, we will follow some smaller recipes and then the pizza will come together right at the end.

Ingredients:

Garlic Oil:

- 3 Tbsp olive oil
- 1 clove garlic, minced

Instructions:

1. In a small pan, heat olive oil over low heat and add garlic. Sauté for about 4 minutes, until garlic is fragrant and golden. Make sure not to burn the garlic.

Vegan Parmesan:

- 1/2 cup toasted sesame seeds
- 2 Tbsp nutritional yeast
- 1/4 tsp sea salt

Instructions:

1. Toast sesame seeds in a nonstick pan over medium-high heat until fragrant and golden (not brown). Add sesame seeds, nutritional yeast and salt to a blender or food processor and blend/process for 30 seconds. Set aside.

Vegan Pesto:

- Vegan Parmesan (ingredients above)
- 6 Tbsp raw cashews
- 4 cups fresh basil leaves, roughly chopped
- Juice of 1 lemon
- 1 cup olive oil
- Two small handfuls of fresh spinach
- 4 cloves garlic

- 1 tsp salt

Instructions:

1. Add cashews and olive oil to a food processor and process until smooth. Then add in the garlic, vegan Parmesan, lemon juice and process again until smooth. Then add in the basil and spinach and process again. Set aside.

Roasted Vegetable Topping

- 2 plum tomatoes, diced
- 1 red onion, diced
- 1 small yellow onion, diced
- 4 basil leaves, chopped finely
- 3 tbsp olive oil
- 1/2 Tbsp balsamic vinegar
- Salt, to taste
- 2 garlic cloves, minced

Instructions:

1. Preheat oven to 375 degrees.
2. In an oiled roasting pan or rimmed baking sheet, toss together the tomatoes, red and yellow onions, basil, oil, salt, vinegar and garlic.
3. Bake for 35 minutes, stirring periodically. Remove from oven and set aside.

Assemble & Grill Your Pizza:

Preheat your grill to high. They key to great pizza is high heat. Ideally, you want the temperature to be 550 to 600 degrees.

Roll out your dough and brush the bottom with olive oil.

Place oil-side down on the grill and cook, uncovered, for about 3 minutes, so that the dough sets. Remove from the grill.

Generously brush the top of your dough with the Garlic Oil. Then layer on the Vegan Pesto. Then pile on the Roasted Veggies, and top with the Vegan Parmesan. Pop the pizza back on the grill and cook, covered, for 3-5 minutes. Keep close - if you start to smell the crust burning, take off the lid and see if you need to remove.

Remove from heat, cut and serve warm.

Bourbon Maple Baked Beans

This is a tasty dish, a sweet and thick bean side. Something about brown sugar, molasses and bourbon just feels like home to me.

Ingredients:

For the Sauce:

- 1/4 cup BBQ sauce
- 1/4 cup ketchup
- 2 Tbsp light brown sugar
- 1 Tbsp tomato paste
- 1 Tbsp light molasses
- 1 Tbsp bourbon whiskey
- 1 tsp soy sauce
- 1/2 tsp chili powder
- 1/4 tsp ground cumin
- 1/4 tsp salt
- 1/4 tsp black pepper

The Rest:

- 2 15-oz cans of great northern beans, rinsed and drained
- 1/2 Tbsp margarine
- 1/2 yellow onion, finely diced
- 1 clove garlic, minced
- 4 strips vegan bacon (optional), cooked according to package instructions until crispy, and chopped up

Instructions:

1. Combine the sauce ingredients in a bowl and whisk until well-combined.
2. In a medium pot over medium heat, add your margarine. Add in onion and garlic and cook about 4 minutes, until softened and fragrant.
3. Add your sauce to the pot and bring to a boil. Then reduce to a simmer over low heat and stir in the beans and vegan bacon (if using). Cook, covered, for 20 minutes, stirring occasionally.
4. Serve warm.

Halloumi Chili

Ingredients:

- 400g halloumi cheese
- 15g red onions
- 300 g strawberries
- 10g basil leaves
- 1/2 red chili pepper
- 3 tbsp balsamic vinegar
- 1 tbsp liquid honey
- 2 tbsp olive oil
- Salt
- Pepper

Instructions:

1. Wash and chop the strawberries.
2. Wash the chili pepper, cut in half, core and then cut into small pieces.
3. Wash, dry and cut the basil leaves into strips.
4. Peel and chop the onions.
5. Put all ingredients in a bowl and mix with oil, vinegar and honey. Season to taste with salt and pepper.
6. Divide the halloumi into the desired portion size and roast for 4 minutes on each side on the grill.
7. To serve, serve grilled halloumi with the sauce.

Sweet Potato Black Bean Stew

This is a nice little sweet and savory stew, chockfull of nutritiousness.

Ingredients:

- 1 yellow onion, chopped
- 1 tsp oil
- 1 Tbsp chili powder
- 1 cup orange juice
- 1½ tsp agave nectar
- Salt, to taste
- 2 sweet potatoes, peeled and cut into 1-inch pieces
- 2 tsp margarine, softened
- 2 tsp flour
- 1 (15 ounce) can black beans, drained and rinsed

Instructions:

1. In a medium pot over medium heat, heat oil and add onion. Cook for about 4-5 minutes, until softened a bit.
2. Add in chili powder and salt, and stir. Add in orange juice, agave nectar and sweet potatoes, and stir to combine everything.
3. Bring to a boil and then reduce heat to low and simmer for 15 minutes.
4. Combine margarine and flour, then add to the pot along with the black beans. Stir well. Cook another 10 minutes on low, until beans are heated through and slightly softened, and the stew has thickened.
5. Serve warm.

Grilled Tofu Tacos

If you've never thought about grilling tofu, well get with the times. Feel free to add some other toppings to these tacos.

Ingredients:

Corn tortillas, warmed on the stove

For the Tofu:

- 1 14-oz block of extra firm tofu, pressed, drained and sliced into 1/4-inch thick planks
- 3 Tbsp olive oil
- Juice and zest of 1 lime
- 1 clove garlic, minced
- 1/2 tsp agave nectar
- 1/4 tsp onion powder
- 1/4 tsp paprika
- 1/4 tsp chipotle chili powder
- 1/4 tsp cumin
- Salt and pepper, to taste

Instructions:

1. Mix together the marinade ingredients: olive oil, lime zest and juice, garlic, agave nectar, onion powder, paprika, chipotle chili powder, cumin, salt and pepper. Place the tofu in a shallow container and pour the marinade over the tofu, Marinate for at least 20 minutes or so.
2. Prepare your grill over medium heat and lightly grease the grill.
3. Shake off excess marinade and place the tofu planks on the grill, cooking about 2 minutes per side, until you have some nice grill marks. Remove from heat and set aside. You can also add some of the reserved marinade if desired.

For the Cabbage Slaw:

- 1/2 cup red cabbage, sliced thinly
- 2 tsp rice vinegar (you can use apple cider vinegar or white wine vinegar too)
- 2 tsp lime juice

- Salt, to taste

Instructions:

1. Mix together all cabbage slaw ingredients and refrigerate until ready to eat.

For the Avocado Cashew Cream:

- 1/2 cup raw cashews, soaked for at least 1 hour
- 1/2 cup water
- Juice of 1 lime
- 1 avocado
- Salt, to taste
- 1/2 tsp agave nectar (optional)
- 1/2 roasted jalapeño (optional)

Instructions:

1. Add all ingredients to a blender or food processor and blend/process until everything is well combined and slightly thickened. If sauce is too thick, you can add in a Tbsp or two of water.
2. Refrigerate for about 15 minutes, until ready to serve.

Assemble the Tacos:

Add some tofu, cabbage and avocado cashew cream sauce to a corn tortilla and serve.

Potato Salad

Potato salad is a must-have at any barbecue. This one is mustard- and avocado-based, but if you are more of a mayo fan, you can add in some vegan mayo too.

Ingredients:

- 2 pounds small red potatoes, quartered
- 1 avocado
- 2 tsp lemon juice
- 1 Tbsp Dijon mustard
- 1/4 tsp smoked paprika
- 1/2 tsp salt
- 1 tsp maple syrup
- Black pepper, to taste
- 1/3 cup fresh dill, chopped
- 4-5 green onions, sliced thinly
- 3 stalks celery, diced
- 1/2 white onion, diced

Instructions:

1. Steam or boil the potatoes in salted water for about 8 minutes, until fork-tender. Run under cold water to prevent further cooking.
2. In a small bowl, mash the avocado and add in the lemon juice, mustard, paprika, salt, pepper and maple syrup. Stir with a fork until everything is well-combined.
3. In a big bowl, combine the potatoes, dill, green onion, celery, onion and avocado dressing and toss until well-combined. Adjust seasonings as desired.
4. Refrigerate until ready to eat. Serve cold or at room temperature.

Macaroni Salad

This recipe makes a lot of macaroni salad. Halve the recipe if you don't expect a huge crowd.

Ingredients:

- 4 cups elbow macaroni, cooked according to package and rinsed under cold water
- 3 red bell peppers, roasted with skins removed, and diced
- 1/2 cup black olives, diced
- 1/2 cup sweet/spicy pickles, diced
- 3 green onions, sliced thin
- 1/2 cup vegan mayo
- 1 Tbsp red wine vinegar
- 3 tsp sugar (make sure it is from a bone char-free sugar manufacturer)
- 1/4 tsp salt
- Black pepper, to taste
- 1/4 cup almond milk

Instructions:

1. In a bowl, combine vegan mayo, vinegar, sugar, salt, pepper and almond milk.
2. In a larger bowl, combine the cooked macaroni, olives, red peppers, pickles, green onions and about 3/4 of the dressing. Mix until well-combined. Taste, adjust seasonings and add in more of the dressing if desired.
3. Put in the fridge and serve chilled.

Beetroot Sheep's Cheese

Ingredients:

- 4 bulbs of beetroot (pre-cooked)
- 150g sheep cheese
- 1/2 onion
- 3 tbsp olive oil
- 3 tbsp balsamic vinegar
- Salt
- Pepper
- If necessary: fresh coriander

Instructions:

1. Peel and dice the onion.
2. Mix the balsamic vinegar, oil, onion, salt and pepper together.
3. Cut the beetroot into thin slices and marinate with the oil mixture. Set aside for 20 minutes.
4. Grill the beetroot on all sides for 15 minutes.
5. Crumble the sheep's cheese, mix with the remaining marinade and pour over the grilled beetroot.

Chapter 2: Vegetable Skewers

Spicy Tofu

Ingredients:

- 1 red pepper
- 1 yellow bell pepper
- 1 zucchini
- 400g natural tofu
- 2 onions, red
- Sweet and sour chili sauce
- Olive oil
- Salt
- Pepper

Instructions:

1. Cut the zucchini lengthways and then cut into thin slices.
2. Halve the peppers, remove the seeds and partitions then cut into 2cm pieces.
3. Cut the tofu into 1cm cubes.
4. Peel the onions and cut into wedges.
5. Alternately stick tofu and vegetables on skewers. Brush with the oil.
6. Grill the skewers for 5 minutes on each side. Salt, pepper and serve with the sauce.

Veggie Kebabs with Basic Vinaigrette

This is a simple kebab recipe with a basic vinaigrette. Every type of vegetable will have its own kebab.

Ingredients:

Vinaigrette:

- 1/2 cup white-wine vinegar
- 1 Tbsp balsamic vinegar
- 1 garlic clove, minced
- 1 1/4 tsp sugar
- 1/2 tsp salt
- 1/4 tsp black pepper
- 1 cup olive oil

Instructions:

1. Combine and whisk the vinaigrette ingredients until well-combined.

Vegetables:

- 1 zucchini, cut into 3/4-inch rounds
- 1/4 cup olive oil
- 1½ tsp salt
- 3/4 tsp black pepper
- 3/4 lb cherry tomatoes
- 1 baby eggplant cut into 3/4-inch rounds
- 10 oz cremini mushrooms
- 2 yellow bell peppers, cut into 1½-inch square-ish pieces
- 1 red onion, cut into 1½-inch square-ish pieces
- 18 12-inch skewers (soaked in warm water for 30 minutes if wooden)

Instructions:

1. Prepare grill over medium-hot fire.
2. In a large bowl, combine 2 tsp olive oil, 1/4 tsp salt and 3/4 tsp black pepper. Take your first vegetable, toss in the marinade and thread onto skewers, without

mixing vegetables on any skewers. Now repeat these steps with the remaining vegetables. You should have about 3 skewers per vegetable.

3. Lightly oil your grill rack, and place skewers on the grill. Cook for about 10 minutes, turning once. Vegetables should be browned (with the tomatoes blistered).

4. Transfer skewers to a platter and drizzle with some of the vinaigrette. Serve with extra vinaigrette on the side for dipping.

Tofu Veggie Kebabs with Maple Mustard Sauce

Another kebab recipe, this time with a maple mustard sauce. Feel free to experiment with different vegetables. Fruits on a kebab can be delicious too. Be creative!

Ingredients:

- 2 medium red potatoes
- 1 cup extra-firm tofu, pressed, drained and cut into 1½-inch cubes
- 1 cup bell pepper, cut into 1½-inch pieces
- 1 cup pineapple, cut into 1½-inch pieces
- 1 cup red onion, cut into 1½-inch pieces
- 1 cup cremini mushrooms
- 1 cup yellow squash, cut into 1½-inch pieces
- 1 cup cherry tomatoes
- Skewers (If wooden, soak in warm water for 30 minutes)

For the Marinade:

- 1/2 cup olive oil
- 1/2 cup lemon juice
- 1/4 cup water
- 1/4 cup Dijon mustard
- 2 Tbsp maple syrup
- 2 Tbsp minced garlic
- 2 Tbsp chopped fresh basil leaves
- 1/2 tsp salt
- 1/2 tsp black pepper

Instructions:

1. Boil potatoes in a pot of salted water for about 8 minutes or until fork-tender. Let cool and cut into 1½-inch pieces.
2. While the potatoes are boiling, combine marinade ingredients and whisk until well-combined.
3. Place all your vegetable pieces in a shallow container and cover with the marinade. Cover and put in the fridge for 1-2 hours.
4. Preheat your grill to medium heat.

5. Thread your vegetables onto skewers, but don't throw out the marinade. Place skewers on the grill and cook about 10 minutes, turning once, until all vegetables are browned (or blistered in the case of the tomatoes). Baste with the marinade as they cook.
6. Transfer to a platter and serve, removing the vegetables from the skewers if desired.

Corn Laurel

Ingredients:

- 10 fresh bay leaves
- 2 ears of corn
- 1 pinch of sugar
- 1 tbsp olive oil
- Salt
- Lemon pepper

Instructions:

1. Boil the corn on the cob for 20 minutes in a saucepan with hot water and let it cool.
2. Cut the corn into 6 large slices.
3. Alternate the bay leaves and corn on the grill skewers.
4. Mix the oil with sugar, salt and pepper.
5. Brush the skewers with marinade and place on the grill. Grill for 15 minutes while turning.

Mushroom Apple

Ingredients:

- 250g red apples
- 200g wholemeal bread
- 1 red onion
- 400g paprika, green
- 1 red chili pepper
- 3 tbsp olive oil
- 1 teaspoon parsley
- 1 teaspoon honey
- 2 tbsp lemon juice
- 500g mushrooms
- Salt
- Pepper
- 12 wooden skewers

Instructions:

1. Wash the apples, remove the seeds, peel and dice.
2. Peel and dice the onion.
3. Wash the chili pepper, cut in half, remove the seeds and chop finely.
4. Mix lemon juice, 1 tbsp oil, diced onion, chili peppers, pepper, salt, apples, honey and parsley. Let it steep for 15 minutes.
5. Clean mushrooms.
6. Halve the peppers, remove the seeds and partitions and cut into pieces. Salt and pepper.
7. Skewer mushrooms and peppers alternately on the skewers. Brush with oil. Grill for 10 minutes while turning.
8. Serve with the wholemeal bread and the sauce.

Tomato Cheese

Ingredients:

- 4 tbsp olive oil
- 300 g cocktail tomatoes
- 4 stallks of dill
- 300 g feta
- 4 red onions
- 1 clove of garlic
- Pepper
- Salt

Instructions:

1. Wash tomatoes, peel onions and cut into wedges. Dice the feta. Peel the garlic and cut into very fine cubes.
2. Wash and finely chop the dill.
3. Mix the oil, dill and garlic.
4. Put onions, tomatoes and feta on the skewers alternately. Brush with the oil mixture. Let it steep for 30 minutes. Salt and pepper.
5. Grill for 6-8 minutes while turning.

Potato

Ingredients:

- 8 spring onions
- 1.5kg potatoes (waxy and small)
- 1 teaspoon coriander seeds
- 2 tbsp olive oil
- 1 tbsp sea salt
- 1 sprig of rosemary
- Pepper

Instructions:

1. Wash the potatoes and cook in a saucepan with salted water for 20 minutes.
2. Wash the spring onions and separate the green from the white. Halve lengthways.
3. Always put the potatoes and spring onions alternately on the skewer.
4. Finely chop the rosemary. Mix with pepper, salt, oil and coriander. Spread the mixture on the potatoes.
5. Grill the potato skewers on the grill for 10 minutes while turning.

Mixed Vegetables

Ingredients:

- 3 tbsp sunflower oil
- 1 eggplant
- 1 lemon
- 2 zucchini
- 2 onions
- 1 yellow pepper
- 1 red pepper
- 500g cherry tomatoes
- 1 cob
- Salt
- Pepper

Instructions:

1. Peel the eggplant and onions. To cut in pieces.
2. Wash the peppers, remove the seeds and partitions.
3. Wash zucchini, cut off the ends, cut lengthways and then cut into slices.
4. Wash tomatoes.
5. Cut the corn on the cob into thick slices.
6. Mix the oil, salt, pepper and lemon juice. Add the vegetables and mix.
7. Alternate the vegetables on skewers.
8. Place the skewers on the edge of the grill grate and grill at a low temperature for 20 minutes.

Mushroom

Ingredients:

- 500g mushrooms
- 4 tbsp olive oil
- 6 tbsp honey
- 3 cloves of garlic
- 1 bunch of flat-leaf parsley
- 5 sprigs of thyme
- 1 tbsp white balsamic vinegar
- 1/2 teaspoon salt
- 1/2 tsp pepper

Instructions:

1. Peel the garlic and cut into thin slices.
2. Wash and dry the thyme and parsley, pluck the leaves and cut into small pieces.
3. Mix the honey, oil and balsamic vinegar with the garlic.
4. Mix everything together with the salt and pepper to make a delicious marinade.
5. Clean the mushrooms.
6. Mix the mushrooms with the marinade and let them steep in the refrigerator for 4 hours. Stir every now and then so that the marinade covers everything.
7. Put the mushrooms on skewers.
8. Place the skewer on the edge of the grillage and grill on all sides at a low temperature for a total of 10 minutes.

Red Pepper Tofu

Ingredients:

- 100g cherry tomatoes
- 2 teaspoons of sesame oil
- 6 tbsp teriyaki sauce
- 1 red pepper
- 200g tofu
- Pepper

Instructions:

1. Drain the tofu and cut into 2cm cubes.
2. Put the teriyaki sauce in a bowl, mix in the tofu and let it steep for 30 minutes.
3. Wash the peppers, cut in half, remove the seeds and partitions and cut into pieces.
4. Wash tomatoes.
5. Alternate the peppers, tofu and tomatoes on the skewers.
6. It is best to place the skewers in a grill tray and grill for 7 minutes while turning.
7. Drizzle with sesame oil and pepper when serving.

Tofu Zucchini

Ingredients:

- 1 zucchini
- 300 g natural tofu
- 4 tbsp soy sauce
- 2 teaspoons of coconut oil
- 2 tablespoons of liquid honey
- Pepper
- Salt

Instructions:

1. Briefly heat the soy sauce, honey and coconut oil in a small saucepan and stir well.
2. Cut the tofu into bite-sized pieces.
3. Wash the zucchini and cut into slices.
4. Place the tofu and zucchini alternately on the skewers and marinate on both sides. Pour the remaining marinade over it and let it soak in for 30 minutes.
5. Place the skewers on the grill and grill for 5 minutes while turning.

Chapter 3: Vegan and Vegetarian Burgers From The Grill

Falafel Burger

Ingredients falafel:

- 150g white beans
- 3 tbsp flour
- 150g chickpeas
- 1/4 teaspoon cumin
- 1 teaspoon parsley
- 1 teaspoon of mint
- 1 teaspoon coriander
- 3 cloves of garlic
- Salt
- Pepper

Further ingredients:

- 4 burger buns
- 2 teaspoons of lemon juice
- 4 lettuce leaves
- 2 tomatoes
- 4 tbsp yogurt
- 1/2 cucumber

Instructions:

1. Chickpeas need to soak overnight.
2. Put the beans and chickpeas in a bowl and puree.
3. Peel and chop the garlic. Mix with the herbs.
4. Add the cumin and flour and mix everything with the chickpea puree. Salt and pepper.
5. Shape small, flat falafel.
6. Grill the falafel over indirect heat for 4 minutes on each side.
7. In the meantime, wash the lettuce.
8. Wash tomatoes and cucumber and cut into slices.
9. Mix the yogurt with the lemon juice.

10. Cut the burger buns open and briefly toast them on the grill.
11. Cover the rolls with lettuce, cucumber and tomato. Place the falafel on top and brush with yogurt. Then place the second half of the bun on top.

Veggie Burger

Ingredients:

- 2 potatoes
- 2 stalks of celery
- 2 yellow beets
- 2 carrots
- 1 onion
- 1/2 cucumber
- 60g oat flakes
- 1 tbsp oil
- salt
- pepper
- If necessary: add 1 egg or 1 teaspoon of locust bean gum to make the patties firmer

Further ingredients:

- 4 burger buns

Instructions:

1. Peel and grate potatoes, beets and carrots.
2. Peel the onion and cut into small cubes.
3. Wash the celery and cucumber and cut into small pieces.
4. Sauté the onion with oil in a pan until translucent and allow to cool slightly.
5. Mix with all remaining ingredients in a bowl and shape into burger patties with your hands.
6. Place the patties on the hot grill and fry for $6-8$ minutes on each side.
7. Cut the burger buns open and toast them with the cut surfaces facing down for 1 minute each.
8. You can combine the burger with your own favorite sauce and other vegetables.

Bean Burger

Ingredients patty:

- 250g cooked black beans
- 1 teaspoon thyme
- 3 tbsp flaxseed
- 1/2 red onion
- 70g oat flakes
- 1 teaspoon miso paste, dark
- 40g walnuts
- 4 tbsp olive oil
- 150 g mushrooms
- 1/2 teaspoon salt

Ingredients sauce:

- 2 teaspoons of mayonnaise, vegan
- 5 tbsp soy milk
- 1 teaspoon mustard, medium hot
- 1/2 red chili
- 15g cashew nuts

Further ingredients:

- 2 tomatoes
- 4 burger buns
- 2 pickled cucumbers
- 4 lettuce leaves
- 1/2 onion, red

Instructions:

1. Mix the flaxseed with 3 tablespoons of water. Then let it soak for 10 minutes.
2. Grate and squeeze the onion.
3. Chop the mushrooms into fine pieces. Heat 1 tablespoon of oil in a pan and fry the mushrooms over high heat for 6 minutes. Then mix in the salt.
4. Mix the walnuts, thyme, oatmeal, miso, linseed, onion, mushrooms, beans and the remaining olive oil. Form four patties out of this.

5. Place the patties on the hot grill and fry for 6-8 minutes on each side.
6. Now use the additional ingredients. Wash and peel the cucumbers. Then cut into slices. Wash the lettuce and tomatoes.
7. Slice tomatoes.
8. Cut the rolls open and brown on the grill for a minute.
9. Mix the vegan mayonnaise, soy milk, chilli, mustard and cashew nuts. Then puree.
10. Spread the sauce on the burger buns. Then place the lettuce, cucumber, tomato, onion, the patty and the second half of the bun on top.

Portobello Burgers

Portobellos are a classic substitute for the meat burger. In this recipe, we put a double stack on each bun, along with some grilled red onion.

Ingredients:

- 1/4 cup olive oil
- 1/4 cup balsamic vinegar
- 1/4 tsp oregano
- Salt and pepper
- 8 portobello mushrooms, stems removed
- 4 thin slices of red onion
- 4 lettuce leaves (I like Boston lettuce, but use whatever)
- 4 hamburger buns

Instructions:

1. In a bowl, mix together the olive oil, vinegar, oregano and some salt and pepper. Toss in the portobellos, and marinate for about 30 minutes.
2. Prepare your grill; lightly oil the grates and heat the grill to medium.
3. Grill the mushrooms, covered, for 3-4 minutes per side, until lightly charred and fork-tender.
4. Dip your red onion slices in the marinade and place alongside the mushrooms as you cook them, cooking and flipping at the same time as the portobellos.
5. Feel free to add vegan cheese on top of the portobellos and allow to melt.
6. Lightly toast your buns on the grill and add 2 portobellos, some lettuce and a slice of red onion to each bun and serve.

Black Bean Burgers

Add a little bit of avocado to these nicely-charred black bean burgers and you're in heaven.

Ingredients:

- 1 (15 oz) can black beans, drained and rinsed
- 1/2 green bell pepper, chopped
- 1/2 onion, chopped
- 3 cloves garlic
- 1 flax egg (1 Tbsp ground flaxseed mixed with 3 Tbsp water)
- 1 Tbsp chili powder
- 1 Tbsp ground cumin
- 1 tsp hot sauce
- 1/2 cup bread crumbs

Instructions:

1. Preheat your grill, and lightly oil a sheet of aluminum foil. You will grill these burgers on the foil, not directly on the grill.
2. In a bowl, mash the black beans with a fork or potato masher until you have a nice paste.
3. Add onion, garlic and bell pepper to your food processor and process until finely chopped. Stir into your bowl of mashed beans.
4. In a separate small bowl, combine flax egg, chili powder, cumin and hot sauce. Stir into the bean and veggie mixture until well-combined, the stir in the bread crumbs as well.
5. Divide into four patties and place on the foil.
6. Cook burgers 7-8 minutes on each side, and serve on a bun with lettuce, tomato, avocado, red onion, or whatever else you're into.

Lentil Burgers

Lentils make for a fantastic veggie burger too, filled with protein and dietary fiber.

Ingredients:

- 3/4 cup brown lentils, rinsed and drained
- 1 3/4 cups plus 1 Tbsp vegetable broth (or water)
- 2 tsp olive oil
- 1 red onion, half finely chopped and half thinly sliced
- Juice of 1/2 lemon
- Kosher salt
- 8 ounces fresh baby spinach
- 2 cloves garlic, minced
- Pepper
- 1/2 tsp ground cumin
- 1 cup whole-wheat breadcrumbs
- 1/2 cup walnuts, toasted and finely chopped
- Cooking spray
- 6 hamburger buns

Instructions:

1. Add 1 3/4 cups veggie broth to a medium saucepan along with the lentils, and bring to a boil. Reduce heat to medium-low, cover and simmer for 30 minutes, or until the lentils are soft and the liquid has been absorbed. Remove from heat and add the lentils to a bowl, along with the remaining 1 Tbsp of broth. Mash the lentils well with a potato masher or a fork.
2. Heat a large pan or wok over medium heat and add your olive oil. Add in the onion, lemon juice and some salt, and cook until the onions are softened, about 6 minutes. Add in the spinach, garlic, pepper and cumin and cook another 2 minutes or so, until the spinach is wilted and the garlic fragrant.
3. Add the spinach and onion mixture to the bowl with the mashed lentils, and add the bread crumbs, walnuts and some more salt and pepper to the mix. Cover and refrigerate for at least 30 minutes.
4. Preheat your grill and lightly oil the racks. Divide the lentil mix, form into 4 patties and spray or brush both sides with oil.
5. Grill for about 3-4 minutes per side, until lightly charred.

6. Serve on a bun with lettuce, tomato and sliced red onion, or whatever else you like!

Chickpea Burgers with Creamy Lemon Tahini Sauce

Chickpeas make a really good veggie burger as well. We make this one a bit Mediterranean, by stuffing it in a pita with some tahini sauce and cucumber.

Ingredients:

- 1/4 cup olive oil
- 4 cloves garlic, sliced
- 2 tsp ground cumin
- 3 six-inch pitas
- 2 15 oz cans of chickpeas, drained and rinsed
- 3 Tbsp tahini plus 2 Tbsp tahini
- 1/4 cup fresh lemon juice
- 1 flax egg (1 Tbsp ground flaxseed mixed with 3 Tbsp water)
- Kosher salt
- 2 Tbsp chopped fresh flat-leaf parsley
- 2 Tbsp chopped fresh cilantro
- 1/4 of a cucumber, thinly sliced
- 1 slicing or beefsteak tomato, thinly sliced
- Hot sauce (optional)

Instructions:

1. Preheat your grill to medium-high.
2. In a saucepan over medium-low heat, add in your oil, followed by the garlic and cumin. Cook for about 2 minutes, being careful not to burn the garlic. Remove from heat.
3. In a food processor, add 1 can of chickpeas, your oil-garlic mixture, 2 Tbsp of the tahini, 1 Tbsp of lemon juice, the flax egg and 3/4 tsp salt. Puree until smooth. Add in the other can of chickpeas, the bread crumbs, parsley and cilantro and pulse until everything is well-blended.
4. In a separate small bowl, whisk together the remaining 3 Tbsp of tahini with 2 Tbsp of water and the remaining 3 Tbsp of lemon juice until smooth.
5. Form the chickpea mixture into 6 patties and brush or spray both side with oil. Grill, covered, 3-4 minutes per side, until lightly charred with some nice grill marks.
6. Cut your pitas in half and lightly toast on the grill.

7. Stuff each pita half with a chickpea burger, cucumber and tomato slices, and top with the tahini sauce and hot sauce (if using) and serve.

Tofu Patty "Burgers"

Another grilled sandwich recipe, this time made with a BBQ tofu patty.

Ingredients:

- Oil spray
- 1 package (14-oz) firm tofu, pressed, drained and sliced in half horizontally (so that you have two flat slabs)
- BBQ Sauce
- Two hamburger buns
- Greens
- Sriracha
- Vegan mayo

For the Barbecue Rub:

- 1 Tbsp dry mustard
- 1 Tbsp onion powder
- 1 Tbsp smoked paprika
- 1/2 Tbsp garlic powder
- 1 tsp ground cumin
- 1 tsp ground pepper

Instructions:

1. Combine the BBQ rub ingredients in a small bowl and set aside.
2. Preheat your grill to medium-high and oil a piece of aluminum foil. We will grill the tofu on the foil, not directly on the grill rack.
3. Pat the tofu dry as best you can and apply the BBQ rub to all sides of each tofu slab.
4. Grill tofu slabs on the foil, about 4-5 minutes on one side, and flip, cooking another 4-5 minutes. Then brush on BBQ sauce and cook another few minutes per side.
5. Toast the buns on the grill, and create your sandwich: spread mayo and Sriracha , followed by the tofu, greens, and anything else you might like (kimchi, cole slaw, cucumbers pickles, red onion are all good options).

Soy Burger

Ingredients patty:

- 100g soy granules
- 40g breadcrumbs
- 250ml vegetable stock
- 1 clove of garlic
- 1 egg
- 3 tablespoons of oil
- 1 teaspoon parsley
- 1 teaspoon dried thyme
- 1 teaspoon dried basil
- Pinch of paprika powder
- Salt
- Pepper

Further ingredients:

- 4 leaves of lettuce
- 3 tomatoes
- 1 onion
- 4 slices of cheese
- 2 pickles
- Sauce of your choice (ketchup, BBQ)
- 4 burger buns

Instructions:

1. Bring the vegetable stock to the boil briefly and let the soy granulate simmer in it for 10 minutes.
2. Peel and press the garlic.
3. Add the garlic, salt and pepper to the soy.
4. Add breadcrumbs, egg, oil, herbs and spices and mix well to form a malleable mass.
5. Form 4 patties from this mixture and place on the grill for 10 minutes while turning.
6. Cut the burger buns open and toast them with the cut surfaces facing down for 1 minute each.

7. Wash and drain tomatoes and lettuce.
8. Slice tomatoes and cucumber.
9. Peel the onion and cut into rings.
10. Cover burger rolls with all the ingredients and enjoy.

Tofu Burger

Ingredients patty:

- 2 red onions
- 300g tofu, firm
- 2 teaspoons of locust bean gum
- 1 red pepper
- 1 teaspoon mustard (medium hot)
- 4 tbsp olive oil
- 3 teaspoons of paprika powder, hot pink freshly ground papper
- 1½ tsp sea salt

Ingredients for chili ketchup:

- 1 tbsp lemon juice
- 90g tomato paste
- 1 pinch of chili
- Zest of 1/4 lemon
- 1/2 tbsp agave syrup
- 1 teaspoon salt

Ingredients avocado cream:

- 2 avocados
- 1 teaspoon cashew butter
- 1/2 bunch of basil
- 1/2 teaspoon salt

Further ingredients:

- 4 tomatoes
- 1/2 cucumber
- 2 onions
- 4 burger buns

Instructions:

1. Press the tofu into small pieces with a fork.

2. Halve the peppers, remove the seeds and partitions and dice into small pieces.
3. Peel and chop the onions.
4. Fry the peppers and onions in a pan with 2 tablespoons of olive oil for 5 minutes.
5. Add the mustard, 3 tbsp water, locust bean gum, tofu, salt, pepper, remaining oil and paprika powder to the onions and paprika. Form four patties out of this.
6. Mix and puree all the ingredients for the avocado cream and the chili ketchup.
7. Wash and dry lettuce, tomatoes and cucumber. Cut the cucumber and tomato into slices.
8. It is best to place the patties in a grill tray on the grill and grill for 4 minutes on each side.
9. Cut the burger buns open and toast them with the cut surfaces facing down for 1 minute each.
10. Brush the lower half of the bun with chili ketchup. Then put the lettuce and cucumber on top.
11. Place the tofu patty on top, brush with avocado cream and top with onions and tomatoes. Placethe top half of the bun on top.

Chapter 4: Fruit Recipes

Pineapple Papaya

Ingredients:

- 200 g papaya 4 sticks of lemongrass
- 8 physalis
- 100 g small carambola
- 1 organic lime
- 15 g ginger
- 100g fresh pineapple
- 1 tbsp honey

Instructions:

1. Wash the lemongrass and cut the sticks in half lengthways.
2. Wash the lime with hot water, dry it and rub the peel off.
3. Ginger peel and finely chop.
4. Halve the lime, squeeze out the juice and mix it with honey, zest and ginger.
5. Wash the carambola and cut into slices.
6. Wash physalis.
7. Peel the papaya and cut into pieces.
8. Cut the pineapple into bite-sized pieces.
9. Skewer the fruits on the lemongrass and brush with the marinade.
10. Place the skewers on the grill. Grill for 6 minutes on each side.

Watermelon Goat Cheese

Ingredients:

- 3 tbsp olive oil
- 300g of watermelon meat without seeds
- 1 red chili pepper
- 1 teaspoon honey
- 200g soft goat cheese as a roll
- 20g pine nuts
- Salt
- Pepper

Instructions:

1. Cut the watermelons into triangles and stick them on skewers.
2. Place on the grill and grill for 2 minutes on each side.
3. Toast the pine nuts in a pan without fat.
4. Halve the chili pepper, remove the seeds and chop.
5. Cut the goat cheese into slices and divide into four glasses. Mix the salt, pepper, olive oil, honey and chili together. Pour over the cheese and sprinkle with pine nuts.
6. Serve with the melon skewers.

Watermelon Halloumi

Ingredients:

- 650g watermelon
- 350g halloumi
- 4 tbsp olive oil
- 1 tbsp lemon juice
- Pepper
- Salt

Instructions:

1. Slice the watermelon and cut into bite-sized pieces of the same size.
2. Cut the halloumi into cubes.
3. Stick the melon and halloumi alternately on skewers.
4. Mix the oil, lemon juice, salt and pepper and brush the skewers with it.
5. Place the skewers on the grill and grill for 5 minutes while turning.

Nectarines

Ingredients:

- 1 teaspoon vegetable oil
- 4 nectarines
- 1 tbsp liquid honey
- 1 tbsp lemon juice

Instructions:

1. Wash the nectarines, cut in half and remove the stone.
2. Mix the honey with the lemon juice. Brush the cut surfaces of the nectarines with it.
3. Place the nectarines on the grill and cook for 10 minutes, turning.

Apricots

Ingredients:

- 8 sprigs of rosemary
- 4 tbsp olive oil
- 12 large apricots
- Chili flakes
- 350g yogurt
- 1/4 tsp turmeric powder
- 1 teaspoon mustard
- Salt
- Pepper

Instructions:

1. Wash rosemary and strip off needles.
2. Wash the apricots, cut in half and remove the stones. Then skewer on the sprigs of rosemary.
3. Place the skewers on the grill and cook for 8 minutes, turning.
4. Mix the turmeric, salt, pepper, mustard and yogurt.
5. Drizzle the skewers with olive oil and sprinkle with chili. Serve with the dip.

Watermelon-Lemon Balm-Macadamia

Ingredients:

- 20g flaked almonds
- 1 kg of watermelon
- 2 bunch of lemon balm
- 1/2 lime
- 6 macadamia nuts
- 8 tbsp maple syrup

Instructions:

1. Cut the melon into eight equal slices. Remove the seeds and separate them from the shell.
2. Toast the almond flakes in a pan without fat. Finely chop the nuts and add them. Let cool down.
3. Wash, dry and chop lemon balm.
4. Chop the nuts and lemon balm in a blender.
5. Squeeze the lime. 2 tablespoons of juice are required.
6. Mix the maple syrup and lime juice with the nuts.
7. Place the melon slices on the grill and grill for 5 minutes on each side.
8. Serve with the nut mixture.

Cucumber Lemonade

The cucumber makes this lemonade a bit more refreshing and less sour. One of my summer favorites.

Ingredients:

- 1 cucumber (about 1 lb), cut into chunks
- 1 cup fresh lemon juice
- 1/3 cup granulated sugar
- 2 cups cold water

Instructions:

1. Blend the cucumber for about a minute, until fully processed.
2. Pour into a pitcher through a mesh sieve and discard any remaining solids.
3. Add lemon juice, sugar and water to the pitcher and stir. Place in the fridge for 15 minutes to chill, and stir again. Adjust water or sugar content as desired.
4. Serve over ice.

Blueberry Crisp

This is a hugely impressive summer dessert dish and is just so darn easy to make!

Ingredients:

- 2½ cups frozen blueberries
- 2 Tbsp maple syrup
- 1 Tbsp cornstarch
- 1 Tbsp fresh lemon juice
- 1 tsp vanilla extract
- 1 cup old fashioned oatmeal
- 1 cup oat flour
- 1/3 cup coconut sugar
- 1/4 cup coconut oil, solid state
- 1/2 cup unsweetened cinnamon apple sauce
- 1 tsp baking powder
- 1/2 tsp salt
- 1 Tbsp poppy seeds (optional)

Instructions:

1. Preheat your oven to 375 degrees and line an 8-inch square pan with parchment paper.
2. In a mixing bowl, combine the maple syrup, cornstarch, vanilla extract and lemon juice. Fold in the frozen blueberries and stir gently. Set aside.
3. In a separate bowl, combine oatmeal, oat flour, coconut sugar, baking powder and salt. Stir in apple sauce, then coconut oil. This will serve as the dough for your crisp. Take half of the dough and press into the bottom of the prepared pan.
4. Then pour your blueberry mixture evenly on top of the dough.
5. Pour the rest of the dough mixture on top of the blueberries.
6. Bake for 40 minutes, or until the top crumble is light brown in color.
7. Let cool a bit and serve.

Peach Cobbler

Another baked fruit dessert dish. Use fresh peaches in season and you will be delighted by the results.

Ingredients:

- 1/2 cup sugar
- 2 Tbsp cornstarch
- 4 cups sliced peaches
- 1 cup water
- Ground cinnamon
- 1 cup whole wheat pastry flour
- 2 Tbsp sugar
- 1½ tsp baking powder
- 1/4 tsp salt
- 3 Tbsp margarine
- 1/2 cup soy milk

Instructions:

1. Preheat oven to 400 degrees.
2. In s saucepan, combine sugar and cornstarch and stir. Add in 1 cup of water and peaches and bring to a boil. Turn off heat and stir for 1 minute.
3. Pour mixture into a greased baking pan and sprinkle cinnamon over the top.
4. In a separate bowl, combine flour, sugar, baking powder and salt. Fold in the margarine and stir until well-combined. Add soy milk and stir well.
5. Drop this flour mixture in spoonfuls evenly over the peaches. (There should be gaps in the covering, which will spread upon baking.)
6. Bake for 25-30 minutes, until top pieces are light brown.
7. Let cool and serve.

Frozen Strawberry Popsicles

Strawberry popsicles - these will be a hit with the kids, and anybody else who loves delicious treats.

Ingredients:

- 4 cups sliced strawberries
- 2 Tbsp chia seeds

Instructions:

1. Blend the strawberries and chia seeds in a blender for about 2 minutes.
2. Pour the mixture into popsicle molds and place in the freezer to solidify.
3. If you don't have popsicle molds, you can pour into an ice tray, cover with foil and stick in popsicle sticks or toothpicks before placing in the freezer.

Grilled Pineapple with Rum Glaze

Pineapple is one of the tastiest grilled fruits. The marinade here really brings out some added layers of flavor.

Ingredients:

- 1 fresh pineapple, peeled, cored, and cut into 1-inch thick rings
- 1/4 cup rum
- 1/4 cup brown sugar
- 1 Tbsp ground cinnamon
- 1/2 tsp ground ginger
- 1/2 tsp ground nutmeg
- 1/2 tsp ground cloves

Instructions:

1. In a small bowl, combine the rum, brown sugar, cinnamon, ginger, nutmeg, and cloves. Pour over the pineapple rings and place in the fridge for at least 30 minutes to marinate.
2. Preheat grill to high heat, and lightly oil the grill grates.
3. Grill pineapple rings for 15 minutes, turning once, until the outside is dry and lightly charred.
4. Serve with remaining marinade, alone or with vegan ice cream or any other dessert.

Cinnamon Sugar Ancho Chili Peaches

This is a unique spicy treatment of peaches, which can be served alone or with any number of desserts.

Ingredients:

- 2 Tbsp sugar
- 1 Tbsp extra virgin olive oil
- 1 Tbsp thinly sliced fresh mint
- 2 tsp ground cinnamon
- 1½ tsp ancho chile powder
- 1 tsp agave nectar
- Pinch of salt
- 2 tsp lime zest
- 2 Tbsp fresh lime juice
- 2 pounds fresh peaches, unpeeled and quartered

Instructions:

1. In a bowl, combine sugar, olive oil, mint, cinnamon, chili powder, agave nectar, salt, lime zest and lime juice.
2. Mix in the peaches and stir gently to fully coat.
3. Cover and refrigerate for one hour.
4. Eat peaches alone or serve with coconut ice cream, oatmeal or a brownie.

Grilled Cinnamon Apples

Yes, apples can be grilled, with delicious results.

Ingredients:

- 2 apples, cored and cut into 1/4 inch slices
- 1/2 cup water
- 1/4 cup lemon juice
- 2 Tbsp brown sugar
- 1 tsp cinnamon

Instructions:

1. Preheat grill to medium heat.
2. After cutting the apples, place in a bowl with the lemon juice and water to keep the apples from browning.
3. In a separate bowl, mix the cinnamon and sugar together.
4. Remove apples from the liquid and shake off excess water. Place on the grill and cook for 6 minutes on each side.
5. Remove from the grill and sprinkle the cinnamon-sugar on top.
6. Serve alone, or with oatmeal, coconut ice cream, or any other dessert you like.

Banana Coconut Ice Cream

It is possible to make a product amazingly similar to ice cream with coconut milk. If you have an ice cream maker, you don't have to stir every 30 minutes as described in the recipe. The bananas and rum give this one a distinct beachy, island feel.

Ingredients:

- 6 very ripe medium bananas, peeled
- 1 Tbsp lemon juice
- 1 cup coconut milk
- 3/8 cup agave nectar
- 1/4 cup coconut oil
- 1 Tbsp dark rum
- 1/4 tsp kosher salt

Instructions:

1. In a blender or food processor, combine bananas and lemon juice and blend/process until smooth. With the processor/blender on low, slowly add in the coconut milk, agave nectar, coconut oil, rum and salt.
2. Strain the mixture through a sieve into a bowl or other container, pressing down on the mixture with plastic wrap so that the mixture doesn't get exposed to air.
3. Refrigerate for 3 hours, removing every 30 minutes to whisk vigorously, in order to introduce air to the mixture.
4. After the 3 hours in the fridge, transfer to the freezer and allow to chill another 3 hours before serving.

Pineapple

Ingredients:

- 1 organic lemon
- 800 g pineapple
- tbsp liquid butter
- tbsp honey

Instructions:

1. Cut off the top and bottom of the pineapple.
2. Peel the pineapple, cut into quarters and remove the stalk. Then cut into bite-sized pieces.
3. Put the pieces on skewers.
4. Mix the butter with the honey and brush the pineapple skewers with it.
5. Wash the lemon with hot water, rub the peel and sprinkle on the pineapple.
6. Grill the pineapple skewers for 5 minutes while turning.

Nectarine Cream

Ingredients:

- 150g cream
- 2 tbsp coconut blossom sugar
- 150ml milk
- 1 tbsp rapeseed oil
- 1/2 vanilla pod
- 1 tbsp honey
- 3 egg yolks
- 4 nectarines

Instructions:

1. Cut the vanilla pod lengthways and scrape out the pulp.
2. Bring the cream, milk and vanilla pulp to the boilin a saucepan.
3. Mix coconut blossom sugar with egg yolks. Carefully stir the cream mixture into the egg yolks. Then heat everything in a saucepan over low heat.
4. Wash the nectarines, cut in half and remove the seeds.
5. It is best to place the nectarines in a grill tray and brush with honey and rapeseed oil. Then grill on each side for 5 minutes.
6. Serve the sauce with the nectarines.

Strawberry-Banana-Coconut

Ingredients:

- 400g strawberries
- 500g of bananas
- 50g desiccated coconut
- 2 tbsp honey
- 1 tbsp lemon juice

Instructions:

1. Wash the strawberries and cut in half.
2. Peel the bananas and cut into pieces.
3. Mix the honey with the lemon juice.
4. Brush the bananas and strawberries with the honey and turn in the desiccated coconut.
5. Stick strawberries and bananas alternately on skewers.
6. Place the skewers on the grill and grill for 4 minutes while turning.

Chapter 5: Delicious Dips

Garlic Dill

Ingredients:

- 200 g crème fraîche
- 5 cloves of garlic
- 200 g sour cream
- 1/2 teaspoon dill
- Salt
- Pepper

Instructions:

1. Peel and press the garlic.
2. Then mix all the ingredients together.

Sheep Cheese Curd

Ingredients:

- 100g sheep cheese
- 250g quark
- 2 cloves of garlic
- 6 stalks of fresh parsley
- 1 organic lemon
- 4 tablespoons of water
- Salt
- Pepper

Instructions:

1. Peel and crush the garlic.
2. Wash, dry and chop the parsley.
3. Wash the lemon with hot water and rub off the peel.
4. Mix everything together and put in a cool place.

Dill Curd Cheese

Ingredients:

- 300g sour cream
- Onion powder
- 500 g low-fat quark
- 50g dill
- Salt
- Pepper

Instructions:

1. Mix the sour cream with the quark.
2. Wash, finely chop the dill and mix in.
3. Season to taste with onion powder, salt and pepper.

Chilli Coriander

Ingredients:

- 1 organic lemon
- 4 red chili peppers
- 150ml sour cream
- 1/2 bunch of coriander
- 150g vegan mayonnaise
- 4 spring onions
- 2 cloves of garlic
- 1 pinch of sugar
- Salt
- Pepper

Instructions:

1. Wash the chili, place on a baking sheet and grill on the highest setting for 5 minutes.
2. When the skin cracks, take it out of the oven, remove the seeds and stems. Coarsely chop the remaining chili.
3. Wash and roughly chop the coriander and spring onions.
4. Peel the garlic and cut into small pieces.
5. Grind the mayonnaise, sour cream, chili, spring onion, garlic and coriander in a blender.
6. Then add salt, pepper, zest of the organic lemon and juice of the organic lemon as well as sugar and stir well.

Garlic Sauce

Ingredients:

- 100g vegan mayonnaise
- 200g sour cream
- 1 tbsp sambal oelek
- 4 cloves of garlic
- Salt
- Pepper

Instructions:

1. Peel and press the garlic cloves.
2. Then mix all the ingredients together.

Aioli

Ingredients:

- 150ml of olive oil
- 70ml milk (vegetable milk is also suitable)
- 2 cloves of garlic
- Salt
- Pepper

Instructions:

1. Peel and press the garlic cloves.
2. Then mix all the ingredients together well.

Curry

Ingredients:

- 1 teaspoon strawberry jam
- 200g vegan mayonnaise
- 1 tbsp curry powder
- 1 squirt of lemon juice
- 50ml milk

Instructions:

1. Mix the mayonnaise with the milk.
2. Add other ingredients and mix.
3. Let the dip stand in the refrigerator for a few hours.

Bell Pepper Tomato Feta

Ingredients:

- 1 clove of garlic
- 180 g tomatoes, pickled in oil
- 200g peppers
- 200g feta cheese

Instructions:

1. Wash peppers, cut in half, remove seeds and dividers. Then place on the grill until the skin can be peeled off.
2. Peel the garlic and put in a blender. Add paprika, tomatoes and feta and mix.

Cole Slaw

This recipe is about ten times better than the old soggy stuff they put on your table at the 24-hour diner.

Ingredients:

For the veggies:

- 1 small green Cabbage, shredded
- 1/2 small red Cabbage, shredded
- 2 carrots, shredded

For the Dressing:

- 2 Tbsp vegan sour cream
- 2/3 cup vegan mayo
- 2 Tbsp white vinegar
- 1 Tbsp grated onion
- 2 Tbsp sugar
- 2 tsp dry mustard
- 1/2 tsp celery seed (optional)
- Salt and pepper, to taste

Instructions:

1. First, combine the dressing ingredients in a bowl. Then add the dressing to the veggie mixture. Toss the salad well, then let sit in the fridge for at least an hour before serving.

Black Bean Dip

This dip will be gone very quickly. Serve with tortillas alongside a bowl of guacamole.

Ingredients:

- 2 (15 oz) cans black beans, rinsed and drained
- 1/2 cup yellow onion, chopped
- 1/3 cup cilantro, chopped
- 1 clove garlic, minced
- 1 jalapeño, seeds removed and diced
- 2 Tbsp fresh lime juice
- 1/4 tsp ground cumin
- 1/4 tsp chili powder
- 1/2 tsp salt
- 1/4 tsp black pepper

Instructions:

1. In a food processor or blender, combine black beans, onion, cilantro, garlic, jalapeño, lime juice, cumin, chili powder, salt and pepper. Process/blend until smooth.
2. Pour into a bowl and serve with tortillas or tortilla chips.

Guacamole

There's not much to guacamole, but get the best avocados you can, and the rest usually takes care of itself.

Ingredients:

- 4 ripe avocados, peeled and pitted
- The juice of 3 limes
- 2 tomatoes, diced
- 1 medium white onion, diced
- 2 cloves fresh garlic, minced
- 1/4 tsp black pepper
- 1/2 tsp salt
- 1/4 tsp cumin
- 1/4 tsp cayenne pepper
- 1 serrano chile, minced (optional)
- 1 bunch cilantro, chopped (optional)

Instructions:

1. Place avocados in a mixing bowl and mash with a fork.
2. Mix in all remaining ingredients and serve immediately with tortilla chips.

Vegan Brownie

Brownies. What's not to love? Bring a plate of these to the BBQ and be a hero to all.

Ingredients:

- 1 cup all-purpose flour
- 3/4 cup granulated sugar
- 1/2 cup natural unsweetened cocoa powder
- 1 tsp baking powder
- 1/4 tsp salt
- 1/2 cup unsweetened apple sauce
- 1/4 cup maple syrup
- 1/4 cup plain, unsweetened almond milk
- 1/4 cup canola oil
- 1 tsp vanilla extract
- 1/2 cup vegan semisweet chocolate chips

Instructions:

1. Preheat oven to 350 degrees and oil a 8-inch by 8-inch baking pan.
2. In a bowl, whisk together the flour, sugar, cocoa powder, baking powder and salt.
3. In a separate bowl, whisk together the apple sauce, maple syrup, almond milk, canola oil and vanilla extract. Fold in the flour mixture until just combined. Add in the chocolate chips. Transfer the mixture into the baking pan.
4. Bake for 30-35 minutes, until a toothpick inserted in the pan comes out clean.
5. Let cool, cut into squares and serve at room temperature.

Feta and Cucumber Cream Cheese

Ingredients:

- 1/4 cucumber
- 1 pack of natural cream cheese
- 1 clove of garlic
- 1 onion
- 200g feta cheese
- Salt
- Pepper

Instructions:

1. Halve the cucumber, remove the seeds and roughly cut.
2. Peel and roughly cut the onion.
3. Peel the garlic.
4. Put onion, cucumber, garlic, cream cheese and feta in a blender and mixinto small pieces.
5. Season to taste with salt and pepper.

Conclusion

One of the most important steps you can do for your health and the planet is to move to a vegetarian diet. Being a vegan does not mean you have to give up indoor grilling. Perhaps, you don't know how to start your vegan indoor grill diet. Take it easy, this cookbook will be a guide for you.

Vegan Indoor Grill Cookbook for Beginners 2021 is the easy and convenient way to keep to your healthy vegan lifestyle. Follow this cookbook with straightforward instructions, encouraging advice, and time saving tips make indoor grill that much easier. Try several of these recipes until you discover your favorites.

CPSIA information can be obtained
at www.ICGtesting.com
Printed in the USA
LVHW110301030222
710048LV00005B/35